ULTIMATE

DOT-TO-DOT:

MINECRAFT®

40 INCREDIBLE PUZZLES WITH UP TO 1,000 DOTS

BARRON'S

Dr. Gareth Moore

ULTIMATE

DOT-TO-DOT:

MINECRAFT®

40 INCREDIBLE PUZZLES WITH UP TO 1,000 DOTS

INTRODUCTION

Key

○ start or stop drawing

● continue drawing

☆ final dot

every 100 dots is a different color

Journey across the world of Minecraft® as you join the dots to reveal 40 varied scenes, from the darkest depths of a mineshaft to the highest heights of the ice spikes.

Visit deep-sea temples with their depth-defying guardians, reveal terrifying ghasts from the Nether, and see iron golems, zombies, creepers, and more as you travel through the world of Minecraft—all the way to the End!

To reveal each hidden image, just join the dots in increasing numerical order. Start at dot one, marked with a hollow dot, and continue to draw until you reach the next hollow dot. At that point, lift your pencil and start drawing again at the next number. Repeat this process until you reach a red star, which means you've completed the puzzle!

Hints and tips:

* We've color-coded the dots to make them easier to find. Dots 1 to 99 are all one color, dots 100 to 199 are another, and so on, so you'll know the color of the dot you're looking for.

* We recommend you use a pencil to join the dots so that you don't hide the numbers with the lines you've drawn.

* If you aren't sure which dot connects to which number, take a look at the surrounding dots. Usually you can work it out by starting at the edge of a dense group of dots and working out what goes where.

* Numbers are always exactly centered above, below, to the right, or to the left of a dot, or at one of the four main diagonals. So, if the number isn't in one of these eight positions, it doesn't belong with this dot.

* Don't worry if you make a mistake—you probably won't be able to notice it once the picture is complete!

* There are solution pictures at the back of the book that show the original scenes from Minecraft.

* Once you've completed the puzzle, why not color in each picture to produce a finished work of Minecraft memorabilia?

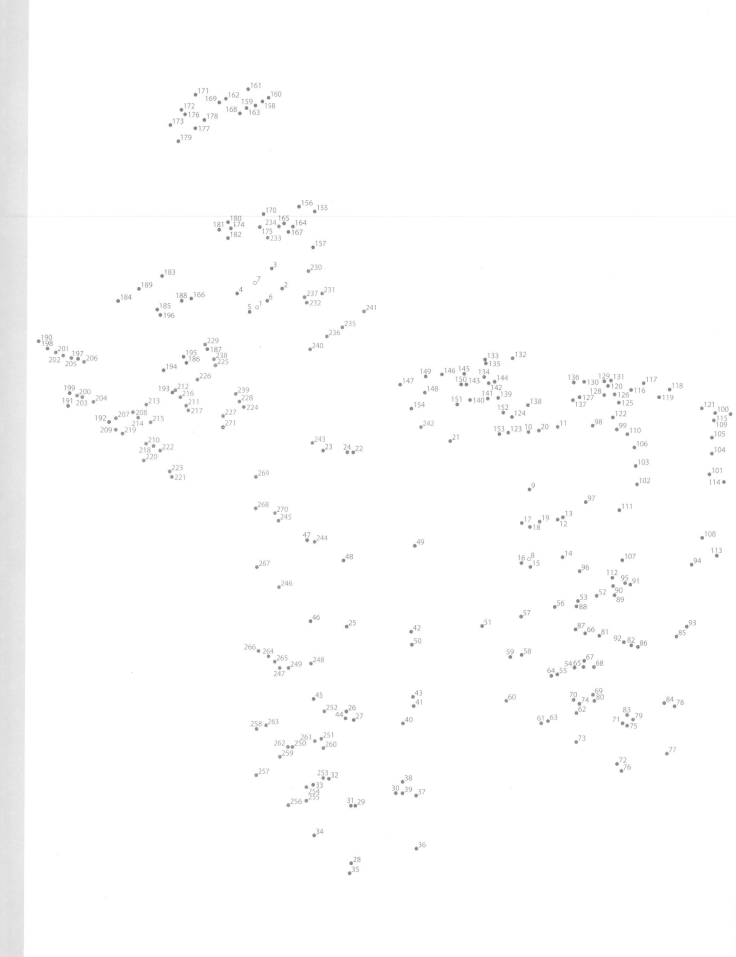

8

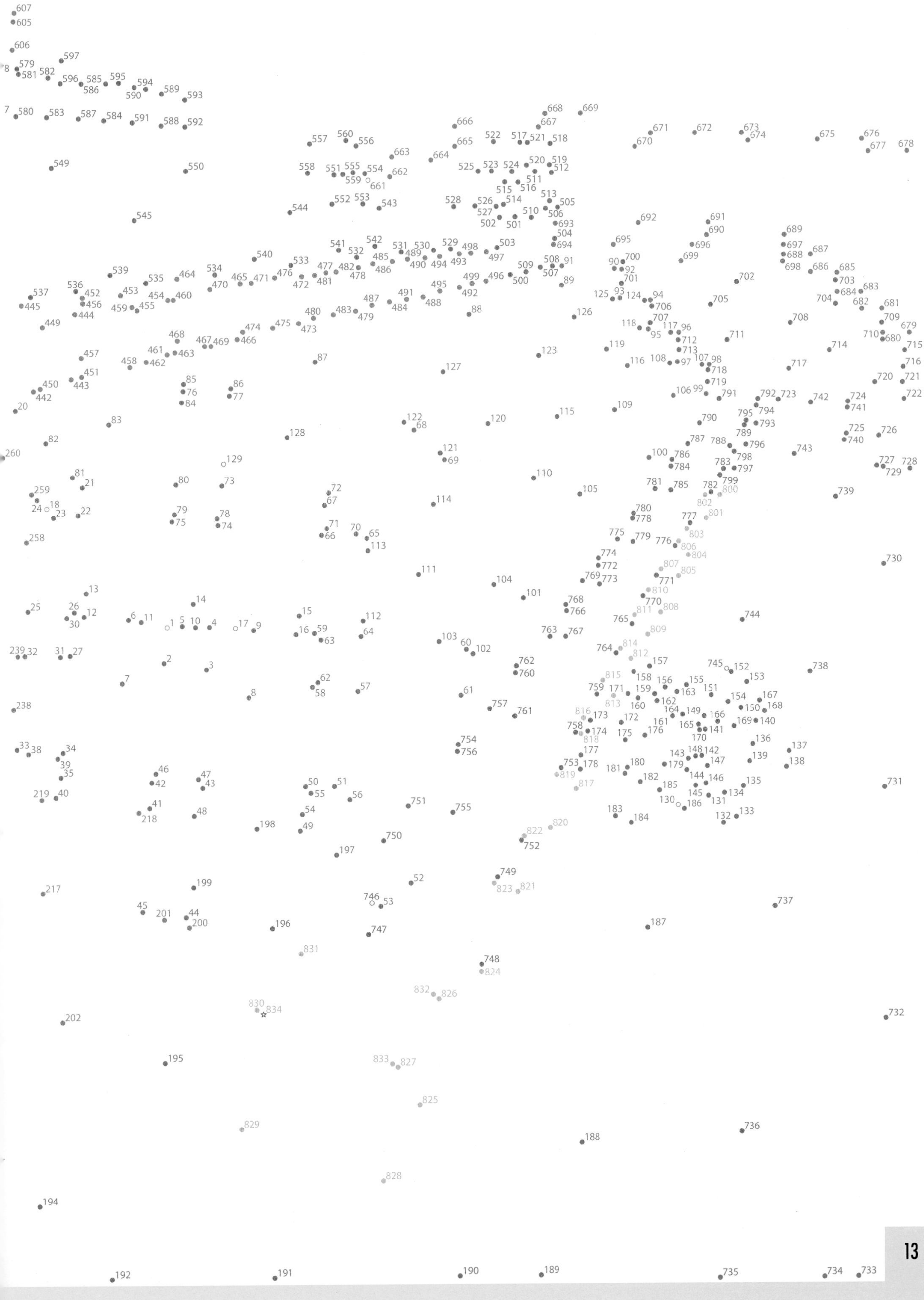

This is a connect-the-dots puzzle page with numbered dots scattered across the page.

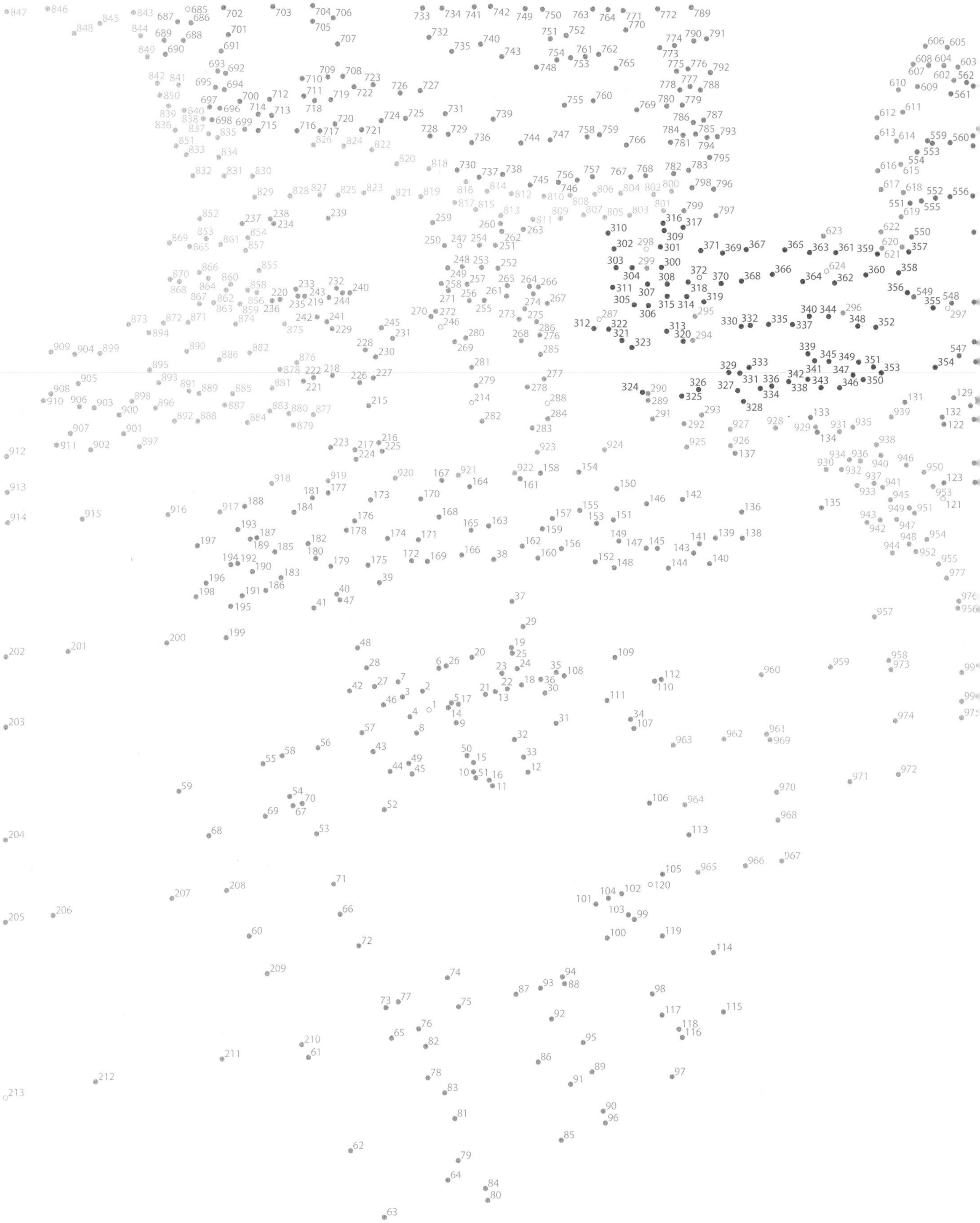

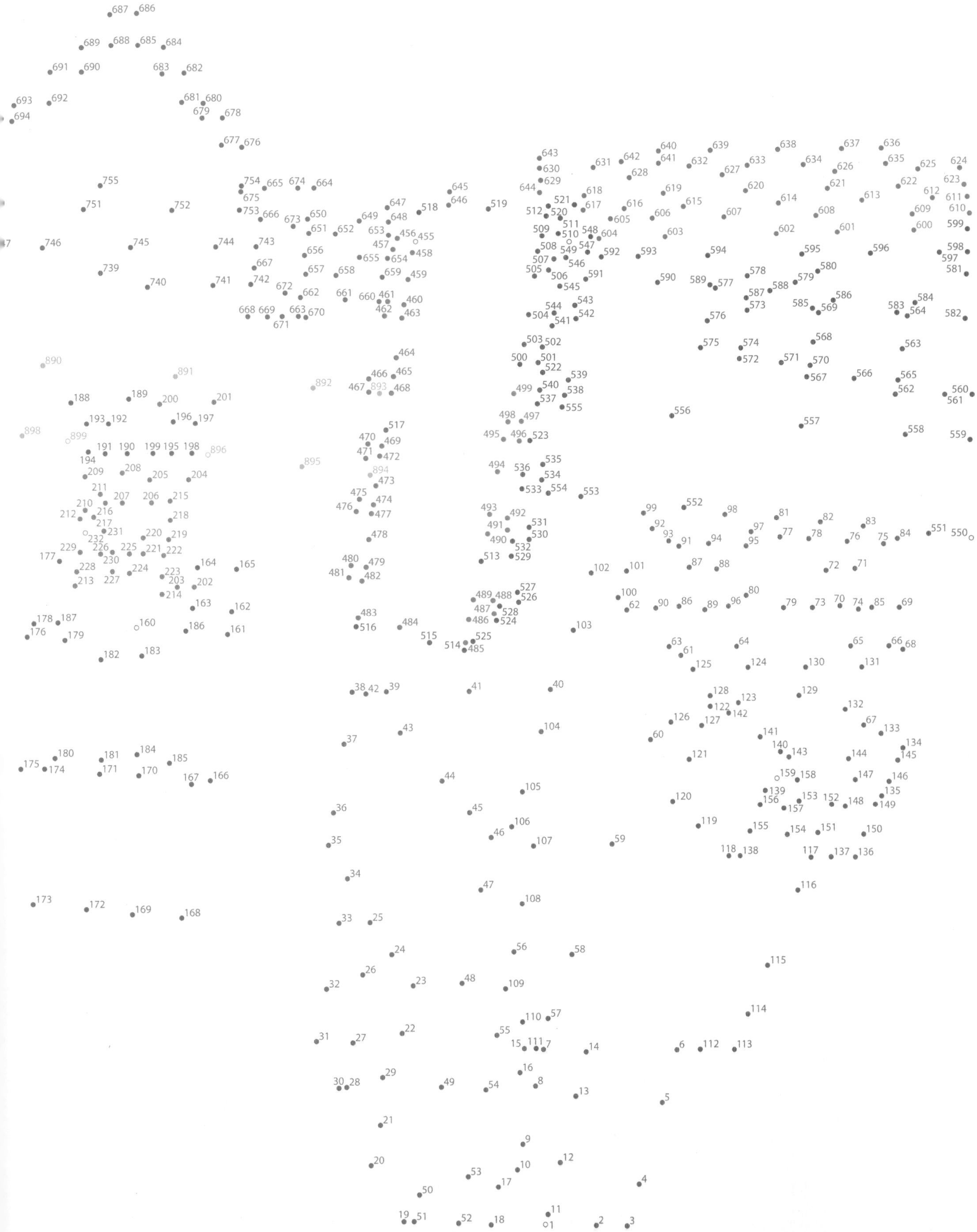

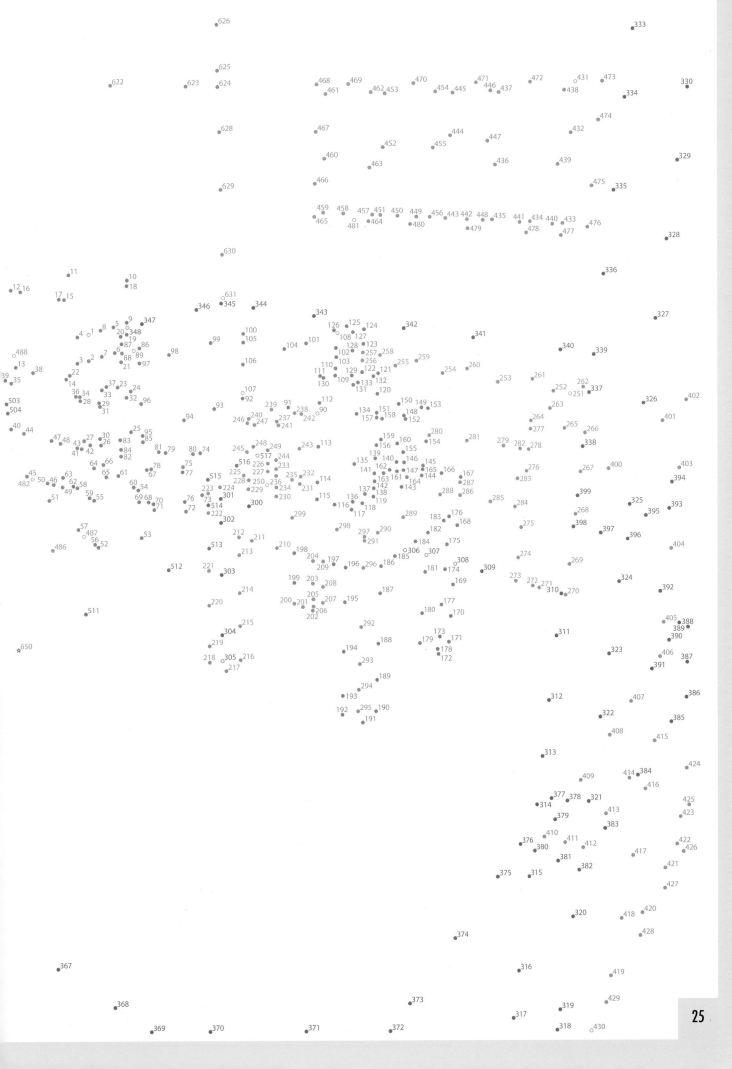

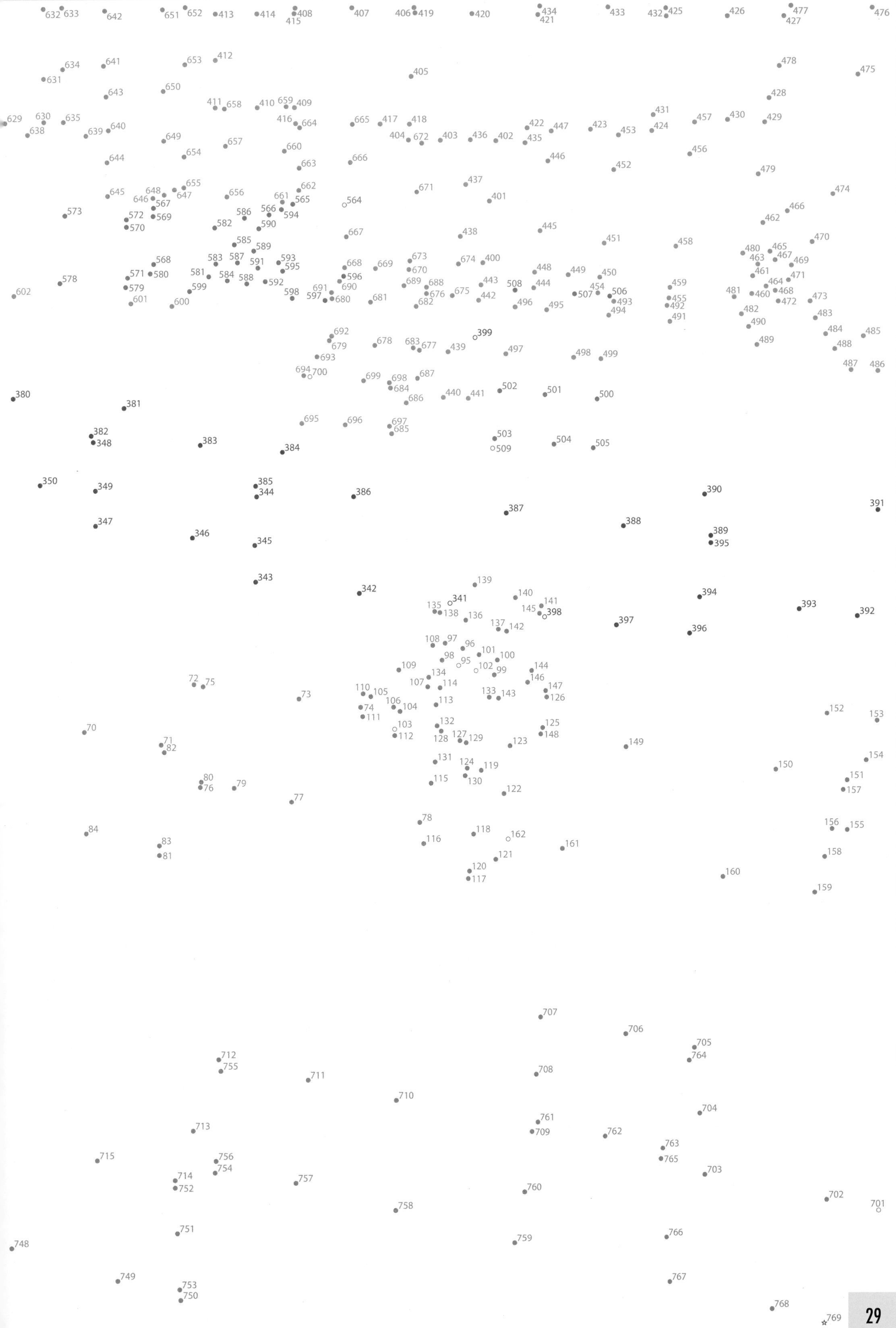

30

43 47
10
22
9
46
44
11
12 45
21
48
20
19
5
1
6
16
17
15
42
50
65
49
64
66
3
2
67
13
18
14
30
31
32
36
35
26
25
23
24
68
51
29 38 33
37
34
27
28
7
8
57
41
39
40
53
54
52
69
56
55
63
58
82 70
59
136
60
129
128
61
71
81
77
62 72
83
135
80
130
127
76
73
134
117
78
84
89
79
85
75
132
86
90
133 131
118
126
125
102
103
94
104 74
116
119
112 111
88
95
87 96
98
91
105
93
122
124
97
92
121 123
113
115
110
108
120
114
101
107
99
109
106
100

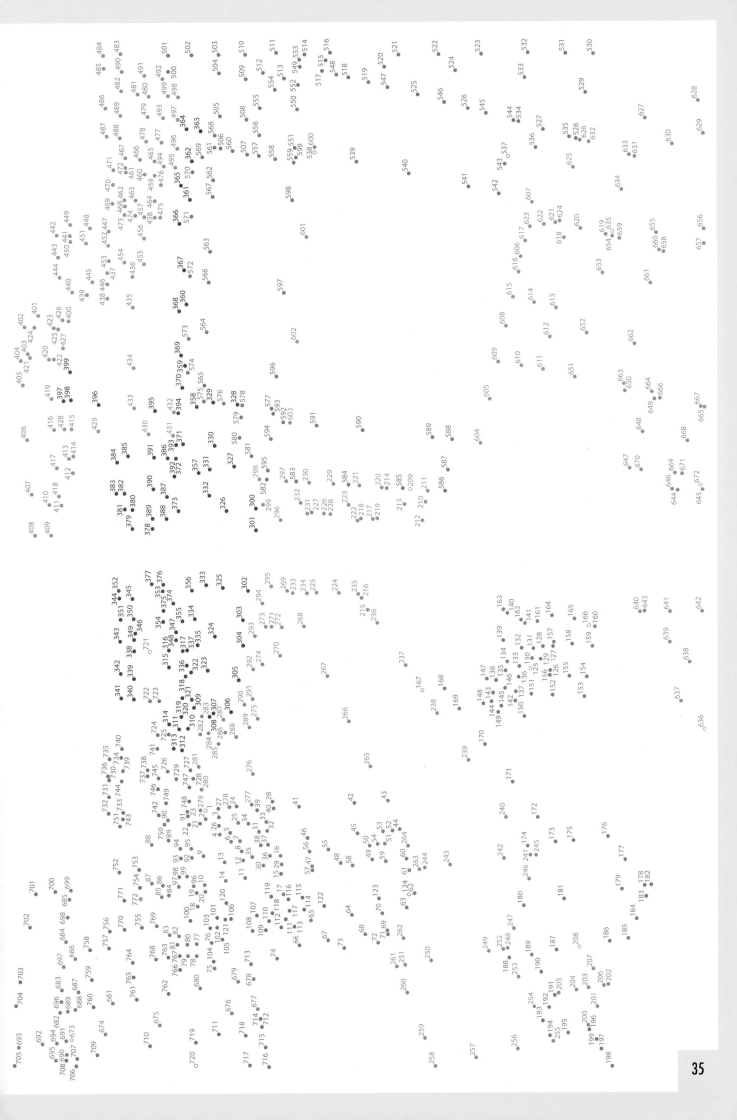

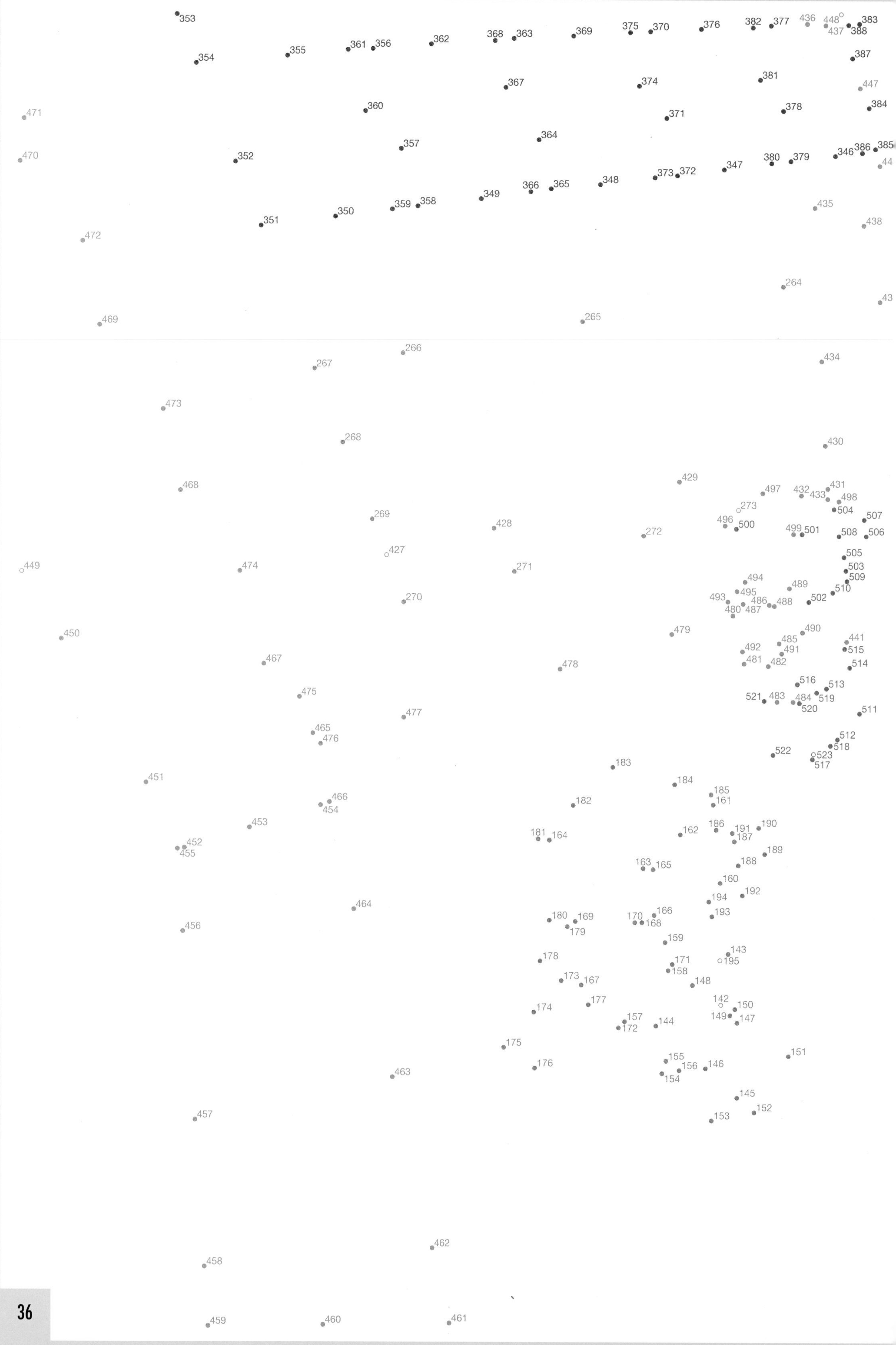

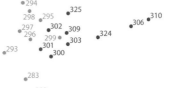
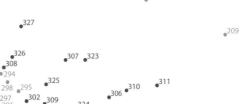

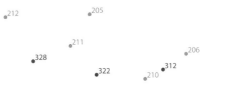

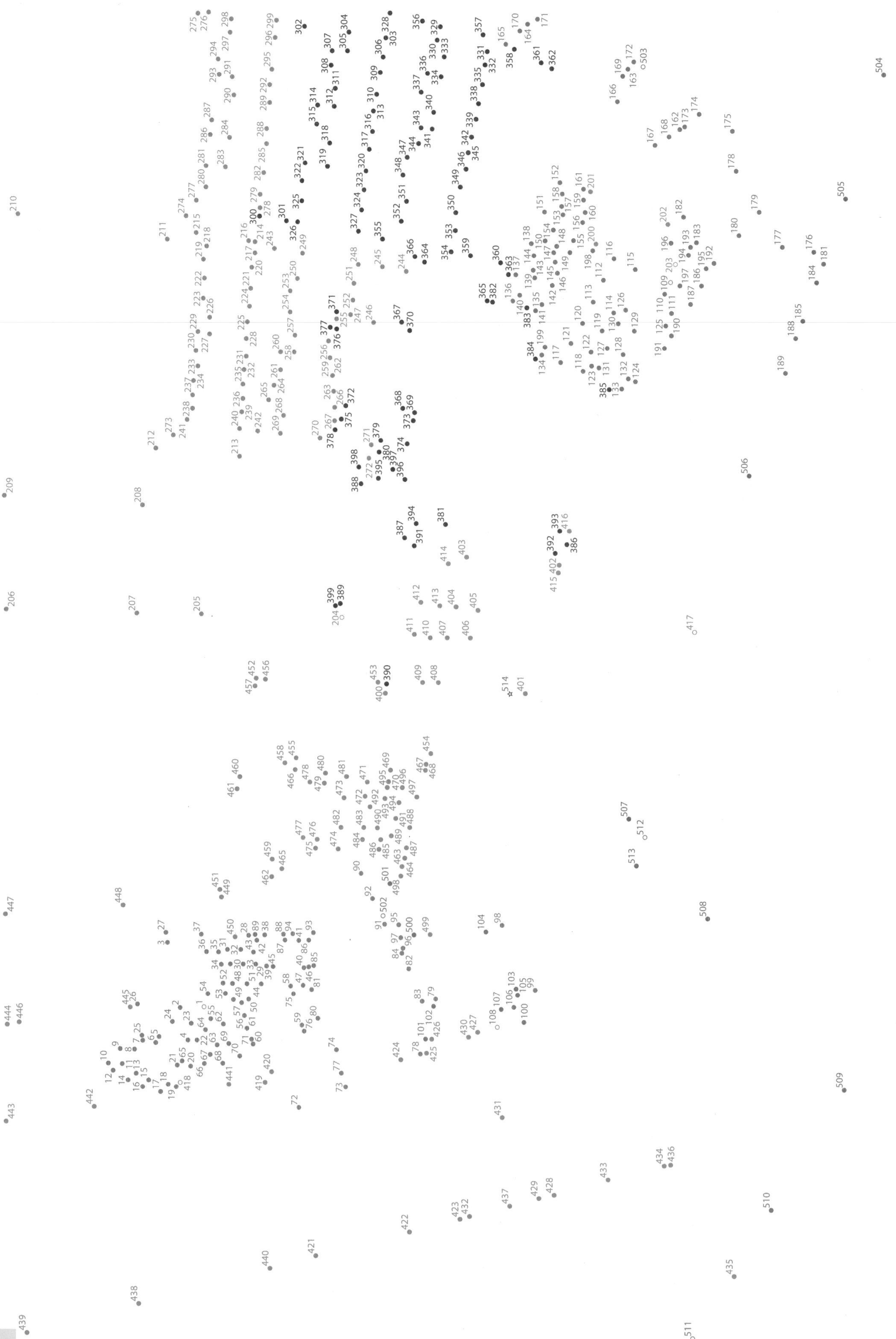

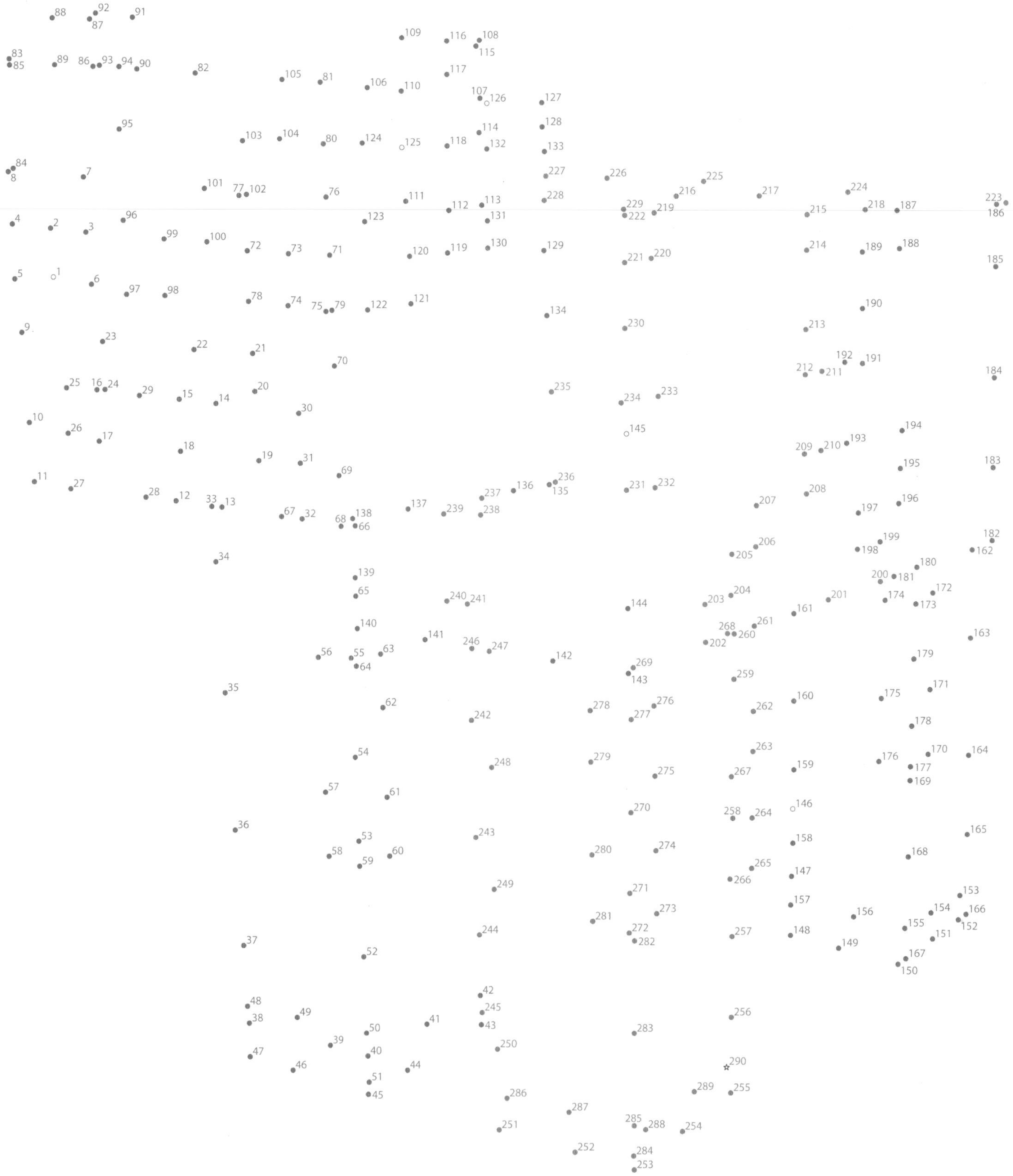

48

51

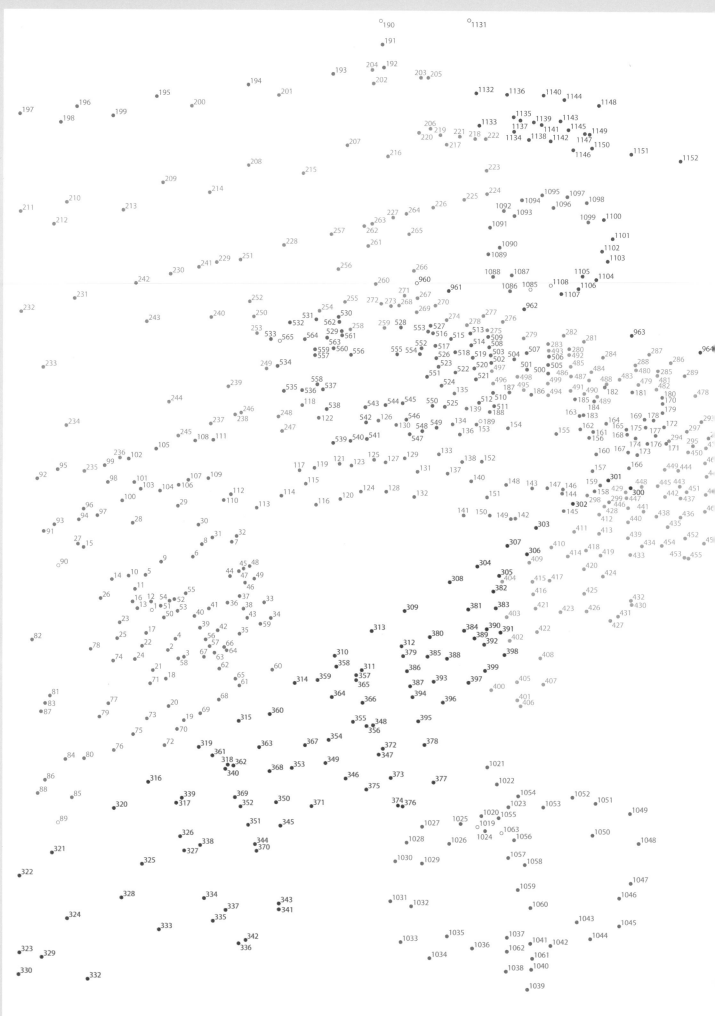

This is a connect-the-dots puzzle page consisting of numbered dots. The page number 55 appears in the bottom right corner.

58

Solutions

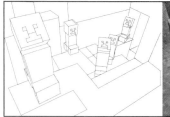

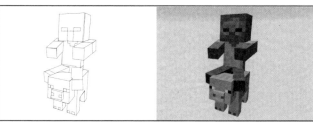

PAGE 4

Creepers are the original mob foe in Minecraft.® If you hear their soft, shuffling steps, get ready to run.

PAGE 6

In Minecraft, pigs can fly! To activate this achievement, ride a pig off a cliff with at least two hearts of damage.

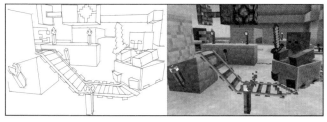

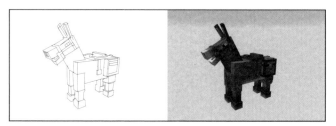

PAGE 7

This sword-wielding zombie is traveling in a redstone minecart.

PAGE 8

Donkeys can be used to carry chests, but if you want to move quickly, look for a horse instead.

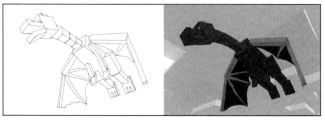

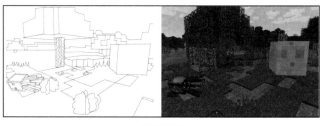

PAGE 9

The Ender Dragon, the biggest mob in Minecraft, appears at the End.

PAGE 10

Swampland biomes are flat and humid. You'll find lily pads, vines, mushrooms, and more.

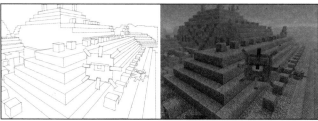

PAGE 12

Ocean temples can be found in deep ocean biomes. They're inhabited by dangerous guardians.

PAGE 14

Crops, such as wheat, carrots, and potatoes, are grown in villages.

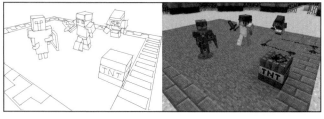

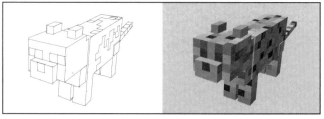

PAGE 16

Strays can be found in icy areas. This one was lured to a battle arena!

PAGE 17

Ocelots can be tamed with the use of uncooked fish, such as raw salmon.

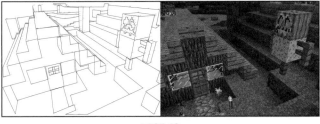

PAGE 18

Jack o'lanterns can be crafted by combining a pumpkin block with a torch.

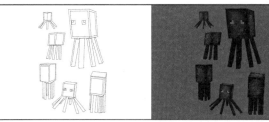

PAGE 19

Squid can be found in deep ocean biomes. They are always passive, and they will drop ink sacs if destroyed.

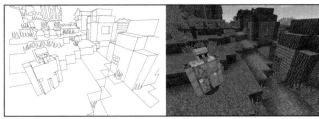

PAGE 20

Iron golems can spawn when a village is big enough. Once spawned, an iron golem will protect villagers from zombies.

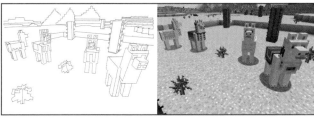

PAGE 22

Llamas can be tamed and trained. They can be useful for carrying chests and other items.

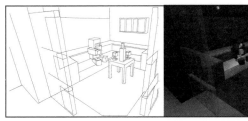

PAGE 24

By using custom block models and being creative with blocks, it's even possible to make modern settings in Minecraft® like this one.

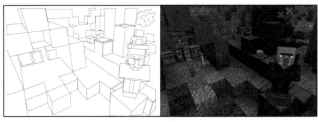

PAGE 26

Witches can be spawned in the place of a villager when lightning strikes close by.

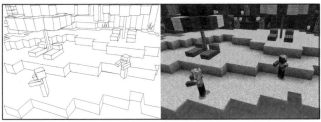

PAGE 28

Husks can usually be found in the desert, but these ones are relaxing on the beach.

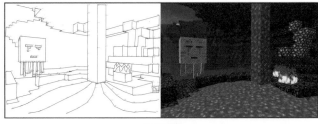

PAGE 30

Beware ghasts spitting fireballs! If you deflect a fireball and hit a ghast, you might unlock the Return to Sender achievement.

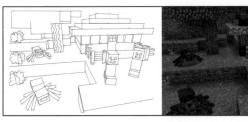

PAGE 31

In Minecraft it's not always easy to get into your house at night!

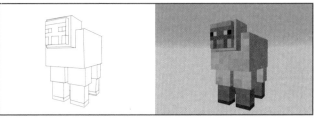

PAGE 32

Sheep are likely to be the first animals you encounter in Minecraft. They are some of the most common animal mobs found in the game.

Solutions

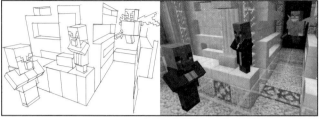

PAGE 33

Vexes (pictured right) are a flying hostile mob that can be spawned in an attack by an evoker (pictured left).

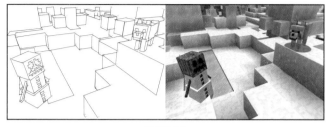

PAGE 34

Snow golems can be made from two snow blocks topped with a pumpkin. They'll melt in warmer biomes and need to be kept away from rain.

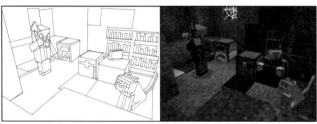

PAGE 35

Mushroom Island is where you'll find the unique mob mooshrooms, which can be milked for mushroom stew.

PAGE 36

You can build your own disco using skin editors or blocks to create the dancers.

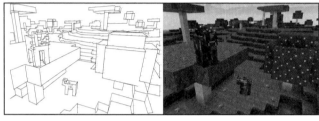

PAGE 38

The desert temple is where valuable goods, such as diamonds and horse armor, can be found. Beware the pressure plate stacked with TNT!

PAGE 40

Flower forests can be found throughout different biomes. Look out for cute rabbits.

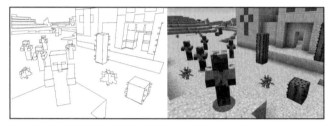

PAGE 42

The vindicator in this scene looks hungry. That ocelot better stay safe!

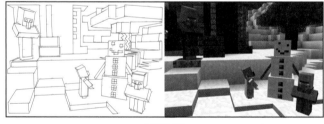

PAGE 43

You can take a pumpkin off a snow golem's head with shears.

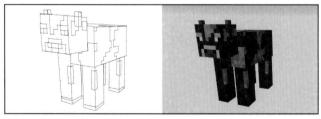
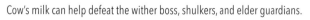

PAGE 44

Cow's milk can help defeat the wither boss, shulkers, and elder guardians.

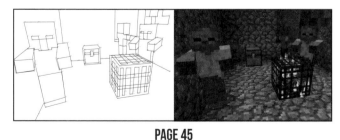

PAGE 45

Dungeons can be found underground at random. What could be inside that chest?

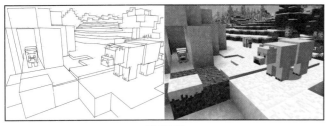

PAGE 46

Polar bears are found in ice spikes and other frozen biomes. They will become hostile if attacked, and they can out-swim you.

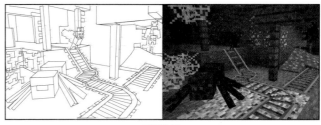

PAGE 47

Spiders in the dark, like the one in this mineshaft, will attack, so keep listening for their hissing sound.

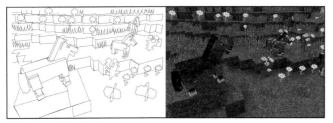

PAGE 48

Horses are the quickest way to move in the game. They shy away from deep water, so lead them through to avoid being thrown off.

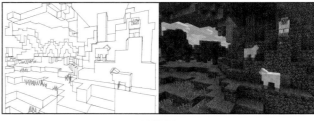

PAGE 50

Sheep mobs can be herded and farmed, and adult sheep can be sheared for wool.

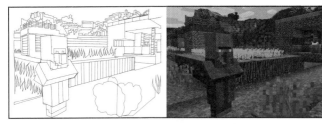

PAGE 52

Villagers in brown robes will look after crops. They will also trade or share with you and other villagers.

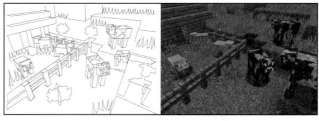

PAGE 54

Farming is a great way to spend time in the game. Animals can be found near villages, where villagers feed them.

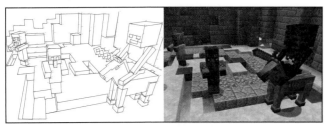

PAGE 56

Wither skeletons are hostile mobs found in the Nether.

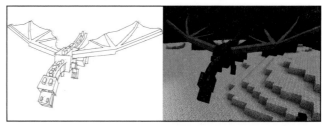

PAGE 57

The Ender Dragon is found between obsidian columns. Once defeated, beams of light erupt from its body.

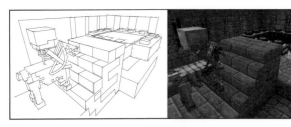

PAGE 58

After you've collected the eyes of ender you can complete the end portal and enter the End.

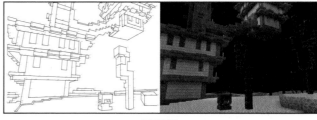

PAGE 59

The end fortress can only be found once you've thrown an ender pearl through the end gateway.

A Quintet Book

First edition for the United States and Canada
published in 2017 by Barron's Educational Series, Inc.

All inquiries should be addressed to:
Barron's Educational Series, Inc.
250 Wireless Boulevard
Hauppage, NY 11788
www.barronseduc.com

ISBN: 978-1-4380-1076-2
QTT.MCFTD

This book was conceived, designed, and produced by
Quintet Publishing Limited
58 West Street
Brighton
BN1 2RA

Designers: Marie Boulanger, Ian Miller
Picture Researcher: Tim Gehrig
Editor: Leah Feltham
Editorial Director: Emma Bastow
Publisher: Mark Searle

Contributors:

Laurie Searle

Romilly Searle

Tim "Jigarbov" Gehrig
@jigarbov
www.jigarbov.net

Jigarbov's Builders:
Bluehush (@thebluehush4)
Ron "rsmalec" Smalec (@rsmalec)
Kovolta (@Kovolta)
Stephen "Faume" Kowalski (@FaumeMC)
Komsjer (@komsjer)
CDFDMAN (@cdfdman)
Carter "Whitherunn" Patterson (@Whitherunn)
Christopher "qwertyuiopthepie" Childress (@qwertyuiopthepie)
Danny "FallenMoons" Moons (@FallenMoons12)

9 8 7 6 5 4 3 2 1

Date of Manufacture: March 2017
Printed in China by 1010 Printing International Ltd